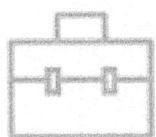

The Gig Economy

Written by Mark F. Magnacca and the team at gigCMO

First published April 2018

Thank you to all my friends and family for encouraging me to follow the gigCMO dream, especially to Ivan, Aleksandra, Lesley and Bonnie for their contributions, and of course my father, mother and my sons for their unfailing support and encouragement.

gigCMO

Fractional Chief Marketing Officers

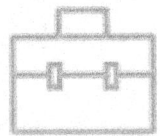

CHAPTERS

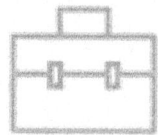

CHAPTER 1: Evolution vs revolution

EVOLUTION OR REVOLUTION? Why this particular choice of phrase to start our take on the gig economy? Aside from a pleasing catchiness, the truth is that these two concepts are very closely connected when it comes to the changing way in which we work.

Has the gig economy slowly been evolving over the past 30 years? Certainly the idea of freelancing, consulting or contracting is not new, people have been doing it for decades. What is new, is the breadth and mindset with which it's being adopted both on behalf of individuals and companies as a result of technology, economy and lifestyle.

In their essay, *Firm of the Future*, James Allen, James Root and Andrew Schwedel hint at an evolutionary change, saying: "younger employees, along with many older ones, also want to work for a company that pursues a higher purpose in addition to profits"[1], linking it to the current flow of change we're seeing in business models.

Socio-economic changes also mean that while employees are more acutely aware of wellbeing requirements from their work and life, that has put strain on businesses to bear a heavy level of responsibility in an ageing society. The gig economy rebalances that re-

---

[1] http://www.bain.com/publications/articles/firm-of-the-future.aspx

sponsibility between employee and employer, proffering individuals the chance to pursue multiple avenues and take charge of their own higher purpose while allowing businesses the benefit of their wider experience and ideas to achieve their own goals as well.

On the other hand, there's nothing like a recession to really galvanise collective thinking and spur innovation, and herein lies the revolution. What had been a mere option in the way of working before 2008 is now becoming the most logical way of working and recruiting, because not only does it make financial sense, but it also provides strategic advantages for businesses, and answers many of the work/life balance questions perplexing the 21st century individual and the brand they work for.

So whether you see the gig economy as an inevitable evolution or a revolutionary change, the result is the same; it's a positive opportunity where businesses can focus with greater precision on the bottom line.

What is the gig economy?

Opinions on the scope, scale and nature of the gig economy vary, with no current agreed classification. It's sometimes known as the 'on demand' economy or the 'shared economy'.

If we look at the genealogy of the 'gig' way of life in the 1920s, the phrase was mostly used by jazz club musicians, which provides a rather nice romantic visual of the concept. More recently however, it was coined at the height of the financial crisis as people cobbled together their own careers by 'gigging' on a variety of part time and freelance jobs.

Then came industry disrupting and game changing brands such as Uber and Airbnb. These took the idea of gigging from an interim measure to a way of life and business by offering flexibility, control and merit-based success to the individual whilst providing businesses with minimised overheads and a broad pool of self-motivated workers in a world where retainment is one of the biggest burdens of HR departments.

The result has been a seismic shift in work styles and business models for both the taxi industry and the hotel industry, which continue to evolve, both providing new opportunity for individuals to earn and giving conventional businesses a sharp nudge to reconsider their market position.

The gig economy has been described as a jobs market characterised by short term contracts and freelance work instead of permanent jobs, and it has periodically been viewed as either a working environment that offers flexibility or a form of exploitation, depending on how it's managed and no doubt depending on your personal profitability from it as well.

However, "over the past 20 years, the number of gig economy workers...has increased by about 27% more than payroll employees" reported CNBC at the end of 2016."[2] In some industries that growth escalated to as much as a 44% increase. In 2016 the BBC reported a 72% increase in gig workers in the transport and storage sector since 2010, and McKinsey Global Institute found that 20-30% of the working-age population in Europe and the United States "engage in some form of independent work"[3]. In 2017 that escalated and Fast Company reported that "findings from Adobe revealed that as many as one-third of the 1,000 U.S. office workers they polled had a second job and more than half (56%) predicted we would all have multiple jobs in the future."[4]

---

[2] http://www.cnbc.com/2016/10/13/gig-economy-is-growing-heres-how-much.html

[3] http://www.mckinsey.com/global-themes/employment-and-growth/independent-work-choice-necessity-and-the-gig-economy

[4] https://www.fastcompany.com/3066905/how-the-gig-economy-will-change-in-2017

McKinsey divided gig workers into the following categories: "free agents, who actively choose independent work and derive their primary income from it; casual earners, who use independent work for supplemental income and do so by choice; reluctants, who make their primary living from independent work but would prefer traditional jobs; and the financially strapped, who do supplemental independent work out of necessity."

What's interesting is that the trend that was born of necessity in a labour intensive job market has been adopted by other industries including marketing and finance, compounded by younger members of the workforce who are entering it with different principles and are either starting out as 'giggers' or taking a view that they will become giggers within a few years.

An ideology that has gained both credence and critics since recession in 2008, it has now moved up the ranks and found its way into the C-Suite, where it has been legitimising itself as a valid form of employment and recruitment. Its roots remain in the idea of being paid for the specific 'gigs' that an individual is recruited for, but the make-up of the gig varies from company to company, project to project, ranging from those who really are in situ for a few days or weeks to a catalogue of 'permanent temporaries'. Suffice to say that as our collective understanding of, and confidence in the concept grows, so will the innovation with which individuals and businesses use the concept to their advantage at all levels of the organisation.

The gig economy is also making itself a byword for cutting out the middle man. It's a world of purpose, without space for tail spend, but it's also a place without smoke and mirrors, making the employee minutes and office square footage work for their place in the budget. A more flexible workforce supported by remote access technology reduces the need for large physical locations, increasingly prohibitive for even the most successful of corporations thanks to the cost of real estate.

In turn, the reduced and flexible office space helps answer the increasing issues of economic and environmental sustainability. As Unilever's Geoff McDonald has been quoted saying - big business can no longer "afford to turn its back on society".

The bricks and mortar structure of businesses has been changing for some time. Hot desking, desk camping and remote working are all taking the place of large, expensive offices with a view of the city. For example, hot desking can cut the costs of running an office by up to 30% according to a report on the BBC[5], all of which we will explore in a later chapter. The changing   ratio between permanent (reducing) and temporary (growing) employees is all part of this evolution.

What came before the gig economy and why it no longer works

The main thing is that our mindset has changed. Once upon a time our fathers, cousins and children all found work in the same big corporation and dedicated their lives to it. The successful amongst us rose through the ranks of one organisation, showing loyalty and a spotless reputation to steadily climb the career ladder in an orderly manner.

Today a multiplicity of experience is an asset to one's career as well as being of benefit to companies. Savvy brands value the experience of people who have absorbed knowledge from a variety of brands to bring fresh perspective and innovative ideas to the boardroom table, bringing nuance rather than prescriptive know-how into the arena.

Short term contracting to garner the benefits of a variety of skills are the order of the day.   Or as one Google VP put it on LinkedIn: "build a mosaic of a career. Just like a Monet is better when you stand back and you see all of the different colours form the picture. Up close,

---

[5] http://www.bbc.co.uk/guides/zgjmtfr

it just looks like dots and blurbs and blobs of paint, but the majesty is sort of all of it together." Who wouldn't benefit from a touch of Monet in their team?

What has facilitated this new mindset? Well it's lots of things. Call it a loss of innocence or perhaps we're all growing up, but in a post recession world where there's no such thing as a job for life, individuals want to spread their income opportunities and have more balance in their lives - time to enjoy that hard earned cash.

Meanwhile, businesses are finding that tightening budgets means that firms are also not seeking to pay large salaries for more senior and economically onerous roles on a permanent basis. So not only are there less permanent roles for highly qualified individuals, but there's less people willing to fill those roles in a full time capacity. Brands that fill up with more junior employees however, still need the strategic direction of experienced team members, and, for example, in the case of marketing, a gig CMO is the ideal solution.

Crucially, the commercial market we operate in has also changed. It's less forgiving and more open to criticism than ever before, and the value of an outside opinion has gone up. This new type of C-suite 'gigger', such as a CMO can add real and immediate value as well as long term value to a brand, and act as an intermediary between inward facing brand opinion and fresh external perspective.

Take, for example, Pepsi's advertising faux pas featuring Kendall Jenner. The ad showed the *Keeping Up with the Kardashians* star bringing an angry protest to a peaceful resolution by handing a cop a Pepsi. The principle was apparently to show that love and understanding solves all problems. In 2017's heated political climate however, against the backdrop of some controversial decisions on behalf of the Trump administration, it was seen as a slap in the face to all those marching for highly charged causes.

Call it a moment in time, call it a phase, but the indicators are all pointing in the same direction; the traditional business model doesn't work any more. While some roles are still best served by permanent employees, the fraction of a company that's filled by 'giggers' is now a legitimate segment that needs considering in its own right. It's more cost effective (a part time CMO can cost the same as a junior member of staff), brings greater stability through innovation, is more transparent, and is a cornerstone to future proofing your business.

Key points

- When considering gig working as part of your business, think of it as a way to help adapt your business to meet the changing demands of the world economy and individual employees.
- Gig workers in the C-Suite can be a helpful outside perspective on your company with a vested interest in ensuring integrity and success of your brand.
- There are less highly qualified people looking for full time roles. Gigging allows businesses to benefit from the experience and knowledge of senior experts but without paying large full time salaries.

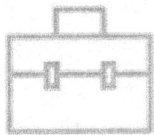

CHAPTER 2: No more Mad Men

AS WITH SO MANY THINGS, the forces that align to bring about a universal change in the way we live and work are many, and to some degree speculative. After all, it is quite possible that historians will never resolve the debate as to which came first, the consumer revolution or the industrial revolution, and we all know how the chicken and egg story goes.

However, in the context of the way businesses use office space and its role in the development of the gig economy we can see a series of trends converge to create a considerably changed, and still evolving attitude towards the need to house employees, and that in turn opens up the discussion around how and why businesses employ people.

As we already mentioned in Chapter 1, we are living in a world where the space in which we work is changing. Hot desking has increased, flexible office spaces are growing in popularity and hubs are very much in vogue. "People are seeking flexibility and shorter lease terms,"[6] Jason Kow, chief executive of Queensgate Investments told the Financial Times in 2016 when their portfolio of London serviced offices was put on sale for £700m in an attempt to cash in on rising demand.

---

[6] https://www.ft.com/content/fd0a13b8-8cb2-11e6-8aa5-f79f5696c731

The geography of which business sectors are located where is changing too. Research into city migration trends, commissioned by the City of London Corporation[7] shows a changing landscape in the city itself, highlighting that while certain industries had a tight community within it, such as the insurance sector, now technology, media and telecommunications firms have moved into the city and have changed the ecosystem - perhaps because of the tech hubs in Hackney and Islington that are in close proximity - but seeing merit in a more diverse community.

At the same time, Forbes reported on the increasing availability of co-working spaces across the world, an industry in itself, from New York to Hong Kong, where "operators offer different businesses, rental offices and desk spaces on a shared floor" and the business model thrives on a sense of community or a proactively diverse renter base to hedge against a downturn in any one segment.[8]

It is a model that Hubble, the proptech company which matches people looking for offices with those who own them has capitalised on, with more than 20,000 desks available and brands including Jaguar Land Rover. "Big companies are increasingly looking for flexible space," co-founder Rohan Silva points out succinctly.[9]

So where have we come from and why the changes?

---

[7] https://www.cityoflondon.gov.uk/business/economic-research-and-information/research-publications/Pages/Firm-Migration-Maps.aspx

[8] https://www.forbes.com/sites/falgunidesai/2016/03/10/coworking-spaces-poised-to-enter-new-growth-phase/#20231062190a

[9] https://www.linkedin.com/pulse/moving-home-proptech-star-tups-dragging-bricks-mortar-age-šuškevičius

In the 1960s the corporate culture, so glamorously portrayed in the TV series Mad Men, was having its heyday. Big spending, lavish displays of corporate wealth, lots of socialising and a sense that big offices were not only necessary to house the staff needed to create and sustain a successful corporation, but it was also a tangible outward facing sign of a brand's virility.

In the 1980s and arguably into the '90s, that model remained very much at full strength, but then something began to happen. As a succession of global recessions left their mark, the attitude towards running a business and looking after the bottom line began to change. The cost of real estate has continued to rise and has become almost prohibitive in the world's leading financial districts, senior members of staff are more responsible for their own communications than they were in Don Draper's world resulting in long-term decline in personal assistant and administrative roles, and developments in technology that have facilitated more remote working.

So the necessity for housing employees in large premises has continued to decline and, in increments, the manager's workspace has gone from a big office, to a pig pen , to a desk by the window, then just a desk, then sharing a desk and then managers have become 'flexi or homeworkers' and bought their own desks.

It's important to point out that it isn't merely economic constraints that have caused change. This is not a story of thrifty doom and gloom. Alongside economic changes, phenomenal leaps in technology, including the Internet, have completely overhauled the way in which we communicate and work. It's probably quicker to send a message to someone you work with by email or (even that is getting a little outdated) a customised internal communications system, than it is to walk across the office and have a chat.

Courtesy of Sir Timothy John Berners-Lee, with a little help from Steve Jobs, not only have the platforms on which businesses communicate changed, "We are all now connected by the Internet, like neurons in a giant brain." said Stephen Hawking, and with such a shift it's unsurprising that people have started to reconsider the physical space in which we work.

Wellbeing and the workplace

Perhaps as a result of recession, or as a natural progression in the evolution of the working culture, there has also been a universal change in the way individuals want to live their lives, with a greater emphasis on work life balance. People are living longer and want or need to be part of the workforce for longer, while there's also increased awareness about the effects of long hours and long commutes on health and wellbeing.

"An estimated 1.3 million people who worked in 2015/16 were suffering from an illness they believed was caused or made worse by work," reported the government's Health and Safety Executive, continuing "in 2015/16, an estimated 25.9 million working days were lost due to self-reported work-related illness."[10]

There is a demand amongst workers at all levels for a different way of working that takes into account their lifestyles and wellbeing as well as financial remuneration. One of the ways this can be achieved is through flexible working. A 2015 report from flexible working experts Timewise and social research charity The Joseph Rowntree Foundation, found that almost half the UK workforce – more than 14 million – would like the opportunity to work in a more flexible way. Meanwhile, The Telegraph reported that US retailer Best Buy adopted flexibility at its headquarters, resulting in a reduction in staff turnover by 45%[11].

What are the benefits to business?

---

[10] http://www.hse.gov.uk/statistics/causdis/

[11] http://www.telegraph.co.uk/business/ready-and-enabled/the-future-of-flexible-working/

The result of this shrinking physical footprint is that businesses now think more creatively and with more precision about how, why and where they employ members of their teams. With changes in the way we use space comes the conversation about a change in the way we contract work.

How creatively can you minimise costs and maximise productivity? Do you need an office space at all or can you be entirely virtual, conducting meetings in hired office rooms and public places? Will you limit the size of the space you occupy by doing as the Japanese do and having stand up meetings designed with the express purpose of keeping them short, sweet and functional?

The confluence of socio-economic changes, technology and attitudes to work means that recruiting gig workers at the C-Suite level not only makes good business sense, but it's a way of life in demand. Perhaps not quite the Mad Men generation but certainly a demographic who have grown up in offices and now want 'out' of the offices but still want to work.

Key points

- Changing the way your employees work can reduce staff turnover dramatically. US retailer Best Buy adopted flexibility at its headquarters, resulting in a reduction in staff turnover by 45%.
- Flexibility is amongst the top priorities for those coming into and rising up through the jobs market, and finding a way to accommodate that is a priority for forward thinking businesses.
- Reconsider your use of space - do you need an actual office or does it need to be as large as it has been previously?

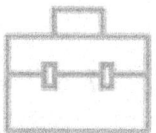

CHAPTER 3: Let the numbers do the talking

WHETHER WE WORK in the gig economy or buy from it, the chances are many of us will have first become consciously aware of it in a small part of our day to day; perhaps when booking a room on holiday via Airbnb or a taxi arriving in three minutes' time with Uber.

While that little icon on your iPhone may mean a cheap and speedy cab fare for you however, for Uber CEO Travis Kalanick it represents the fastest growing startup in history, valued at $60billion after five years in business and spawning a massive change in the earning opportunities of taxi drivers. Is this an illustration of the power of the gig economy? Or is Kalanick the Harry Potter of the app world; a lottery winner amongst a sea of players?

Throughout the industrial era, there have arguably been two areas of employment: the public sector and the private sector. We have talked about the world in which entire families would find themselves working for the same firm with multi-generational loyalty, told from youth that to rise through the ranks of a large business and cash out at the end with a good pension and a medal for reliability, was to be secure, only to have that illusion shattered by fast changing industry trends and a series of economic recessions.

Now we find ourselves in a rapidly and continually evolving world of the gig worker, where the parameters continue to be defined and the opportunities are being uncovered daily. We are living out Bobby Kennedy's dream (although perhaps not in the context that he meant it) and living in a world that instead of asking 'why?' asks 'why not?' when it comes to changing the model in which we work, but who's involved and how many people are actually turning theory into practice?

How many people work in the gig economy?

"The "gig economy" is triumphing over everything else," wrote the Telegraph newspaper, citing the likelihood that the number of self-employed workers could overtake the number employed in the public sector, perhaps before we finish writing this page.[12] Figures quoted go as far back as 1975, when a reported 8.7% of the workforce in the UK worked for themselves, merely rising to 12% in 2008 but then growing rapidly to 16% by January 2016, from which it has continued to escalate. "[the gig economy] shows no sign of slowing down," they conclude, "and it is going to impact the economy and the political system far more than most people yet realise."

Meanwhile, in America the U.S. Bureau of Labor Statistics (BLS) estimated that the trend in gig working had grown by more than 65% between 2009 and 2017[13], and a study conducted by Intuit predicted that by 2020 40% of American workers would be independent contractors.[14]

---

[12] http://www.telegraph.co.uk/finance/jobs/12106318/The-self-employed-will-overtake-the-public-sector-with-the-gig-economy.html

[13] http://www.businesswire.com/news/home/20160615005886/en/Haven't-Bought-Gig-Economy-Survey-Data-Shows

[14] https://www.business.com/articles/gig-economy-trends-developments-and-insights-into-the-industry-2016/

What proof is there that it's going to continue to grow?

Of course, just because the numbers have grown across one decade doesn't mean the trend is going to continue moving forwards, so what are the indicators that suggest this is a phenomenon that's here to stay? Faith Popcorn, CEO and founder of Faith Popcorn's BrainReserve, highlighted the importance of millennial mentality alongside technical progress to *Fast Company,* saying that for this, the largest cohort in the workforce, "the idea of one career seems increasingly untenable", citing the economy they inherited alongside the rise in automation and AI.[15] Then there's the decline in permanent candidate availability because people with the right skills want different things from their careers and to work in a different way: "Finding people to do the jobs on offer is rapidly becoming employers' biggest headache, and many are reporting an increasing number of white-collar jobs as hard to fill, including in the IT and financial sectors," said REC Chief Executive Kevin Green.[16]

Consolidating those thoughts, a study by Ernst & Young businesses showed that businesses are gravitating towards the gig economy because of economic advantages, the greater access of cloud computing and other technologies, the availability of the right talent, and a changing way in which businesses are managed.

In their survey, 49% of large organisations (100,000 employees or more), said they increased their use of gig workers in the last five years, 40% expected to increase their use of contingent workers in the next five

---

[15] https://www.fastcompany.com/3066905/how-the-gig-economy-will-change-in-2017

[16] http://www2.staffingindustry.com/eng/Editorial/Daily-News/UK-Permanent-candidate-availability-drops-at-fastest-pace-in-15-months-41630

years, and a quarter expected 30% or more of their work-force to be contingent workers by 2020.[17] The same survey showed a very high rate of employee satisfaction amongst gig workers, with 73% reporting positively on the arrangements they had with clients and with 66% believing the benefits of contingent working outweighed the downsides compared to just 6% who believe the opposite.

Crucially, this survey shows the changing ethos of the gig economy. What may have started as a cost effective solution for start ups and an opportunity for individuals to earn extra cash in a job poor, post recession market, has show itself to be an interesting model for managing businesses.

Tony Steadman, Principal, People Advisory Services, Ernst & Young LLP said: "the survey responses suggest that organisations are welcoming gig workers as a part of their growth and change management strategies. This gig economy looks very different than the traditional picture of seasonal workers or workers who provide common services to consumers."[18] This is evidence that the gig economy is an entirely different beast to what has gone before in the way businesses use contractors, consultants and freelancers, and as it develops it has the capacity to be shaped and moulded by those who wish to be a part of it.

This is a particularly interesting point, because we have all heard the criticisms levied at the gig economy. Since it started gaining popularity in 2008, questions have arisen about its ethical nature, whether companies are exploiting workers with a lack of certainty and employee rights for example. However, it seems that these are only

[17] http://www.ey.com/us/en/newsroom/news-releases/news-gig-workers-by-design-ey-survey-shows-businesses-need-to-catch-up-to-the-gig-economy

[18] http://www.ey.com/us/en/newsroom/news-releases/news-gig-workers-by-design-ey-survey-shows-businesses-need-to-catch-up-to-the-gig-economy

natural questions which, far from highlighting weaknesses in the concept, are evidence that it is being taken seriously and is refining its parameters to be a longstanding, legitimate way of working and recruiting.

Which industries and skillsets make up the gig economy?

What started in the service sector with taxis and tourism is now a model that applies across almost all areas of industry. We're seeing the gig economy morph into something that's applicable and utilised across all job levels and industry types from copywriters to CMOs. Data to show exactly which sectors have the biggest proportions of gig workers are hard to quantify, but the Bureau of Labor Statistics in the States has said that between "2003 and 2013, all industry sectors experienced growth in non-employer businesses."[19] While the earliest incarnation of the gig economy has largely leant itself to on demand services, it is assertions like that in EY's survey that indicate growth in the gig economy across all sectors whether it be finance, marketing, tourism, engineering, or anything else. In short, there doesn't seem to be a cap on the possibilities for gig working be that in terms of industry sector or rank and file; it is up to individuals and businesses to make it work for them.

Key points

- For those coming into the job market, there is a different mindset about careers; many will envisage having multiple careers over their lifetime - how is your organisation preparing to accommodate a changing mindset?
- People want different things from their jobs, including a greater work life balance, they are no longer satisfied

[19] https://www.bls.gov/careeroutlook/2016/article/what-is-the-gig-economy.htm

simply with financial remuneration. How are you and your HR policies going to accommodate that?
- The gig economy now spans all business sectors - consider which parts of your business might really benefit from a gig approach and use it strategically.

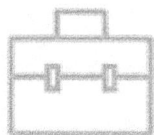

CHAPTER 4: The gig trajectory

THE OFFICES have changed, the customers have changed, the lifestyle requirements have changed and the technology has changed, so what of the C Suite? How has that changed amidst the rise of the gig economy, and how can a new way of operating at board level be used to adapt business models to those that will continue to thrive in an ever evolving environment?

"As we move from the "Fordist" era of mass production into the entrepreneurial age, the future of the social compact in developed economies depends on rethinking the role and nature of many institutions," commented the Financial Times.[20] The article in question took by way of example the changing requirements of welfare and how new ways of working could redefine the perimeters of assessing and managing risk. In short, it's not just businesses that are changing, it's whole industries.

What did the old C-Suite look like?

The traditional C-Suite was a product of the big companies, bigger spend, Mad Men glamour model that

---

[20] https://www.ft.com/content/
a642d4ae-4169-11e7-82b6-896b95f30f58

we have previously talked about. Big glass offices and bigger pay cheques, a longstanding commitment to industry that resulted in a seat at the biggest table in the tallest office.

Twenty years ago the tenure of a board level employee may have been as long as a decade, and to an extent this is still a model that remains in some well established companies that dominate the FTSE 100/250 or the Dow Jones 30, those which are arguably the most stable courtesy of their long term positioning. However, things have changed and are continuing to change, new businesses are joining the market and fast, and with them there's a change in the boardroom. In fact, the interim Management Association (IMA) reported that the use of interim workers at a senior level increased 93% between 2006 and 2016 with indications implying that those numbers are set to increase, citing it as "a growing market... reportedly worth £2 billion."

What's new in the C-Suite?

Today we find that the average tenure of C-Suite executives is rapidly falling. For example, the Wall Street Journal reported in March 2017 that the duration of the roles in America's biggest brands had continued to fall for another consecutive year: "a study of CMOs from 100 of the top U.S. ad spenders found that the average tenure for marketing czars fell to 42 months in 2016, down from 44 months in 2015."[21]

Greg Welch, a consultant in executive search firm Spencer Stuart cited "tough business headwinds, new technologies and pressures to change quickly" as instrumental in the many reasons for the churn.

It is in the role of the CMO in particular that this level of change is particularly high compared to the longer average tenure of CFOs and CEOs for example, largely

---

[21] https://www.wsj.com/articles/average-tenure-of-cmo-continues-to-decline-1489777765

due to the exceptionally high pressures to produce results in a short space of time. However, across the spectrum of C-Suite roles, the average tenure was 5.3 years according to research from Korn Ferry[22].

Why the change?

Well, there are the points we have already covered - the changing technologies, lifestyles and economy in which we are all functioning, which have lead to new opportunities and the chance to think differently about the way we work. Those changes apply to all sizes of business, and the changing duration of tenure is testament to the way those elements are playing out.

Then there's crisis management. The C-Suite is under more pressure than ever to show high company performance, and this in itself is a reason for the increasing churn. In 2015 Twitter surprised Silicon Valley and Wall Street when CEO Dick Costolo announced he would be stepping down and installing an interim CEO in the form of co founder Jack Dorsey, due to flat growth that year. Business Insider UK reported, "a company's decision to put up an interim CEO during a time of crisis is fairly common" and "in the Strategic Management Journal, University of Virginia professors Gary A. Ballinger and Jeremy J. Marcel found that about 17% of CEO successions of public companies install an interim CEO for 45 days or more before settling on a permanent one."[23]

Meanwhile there has also been a huge rise in entrepreneurship, and this has a different reason for utilising gig workers at C-Suite level. Developments in technology, financing and corporate culture have lead to a rise in the power and leverage of small companies. Unlike their

---

[22] https://www.marketingprofs.com/charts/2017/31713/the-average-age-and-tenure-of-c-suite-executives

[23] http://uk.businessinsider.com/why-companies-use-interim-ceos-2015-6?r=US&IR=T

larger counterparts, they tend to be more agile and adept at using the available resources we have previously spoken about - hubs, cloud based working, and a less physical presence and they have different requirements of their senior executives because they have very specific targets for different growth phases. As Fortune puts it: "empowered entrepreneurs can adapt and execute fast, expanding nimbly at co-working spaces and benefiting from the increasing pool of flexible talent."[24]

For these fast growing businesses the C-Suite requirements lie in the need for guidance. While technological and innovative thinking may be in hand with younger members of the team, it is the requirement of senior executives to guide that talent into greater profit and growth.

"We know that different times and different circumstances call for different leadership skills" commented the Harvard Business Review, continuing: "once people reach the C-suite, technical and functional expertise matters less than leadership skills and a strong grasp of business fundamentals."[25] The statement came from an examination of executive profiles developed over the past decade by the executive search firm Heidrick & Struggles. The requirement, it seems, is short term advisory roles at C-Suite level, thus lending itself to a selection of gig style board members with targeted remits for different phases, rather than permanent senior members of the team.

What companies can take from this knowledge

What we're seeing emerge is an opportunity to rethink business models with a view to future proofing companies of all sizes. Big corporations are starting to look at the options that are proving to have great benefit in a

---

[24] http://fortune.com/2014/06/12/behind-the-rise-of-entrepreneurship/

[25] https://hbr.org/2011/03/the-new-path-to-the-c-suite

rapidly growing new generation of businesses, and see what can be learned from them.

These are questions that apply to all businesses - what technologies are available to you? How is your business and the demographic of your clients changing? What function are particular roles performing in your company? Where is your business now? Where do you want it to go? How, or perhaps more accurately, who, is going to get you there? And when you've asked all those questions consider - is it one team that's going to be able to meet all those requirements, or could a composition of gig C-Suite executives with different experiences and knowledge be a more powerful resource for the things you want to achieve?

Key points

- Younger companies are adopting policies of bringing in short term C-Suite executives to navigate particular growth phases and help meet specific targets. Consider the benefits of a senior member of staff joining your team on a gig basis to help drive your company forwards at particular times.
- Consider the position of some of Silicon Valley's most successful businesses - adapting quickly and flexibly with the help of shared office spaces and a pool of talent from which to draw on when needed.
- Consider what you want to achieve within your organisation and the function you need particular roles to perform within that to ascertain whether a gig approach might be the most productive.

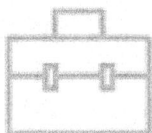

CHAPTER 5: The successful gig mindset

WE HAVE TALKED a lot about the hard realities of the gig economy - how it came into being and how changes in the socio economic environment have provided the right climate for it to grow and evolve. Having established all of that however, it's important to look at the mindset of the successful gig employee and how that mindset is integral to adding value to your business. After all, it's not simply about selecting someone with a good CV and putting them into a temporary role.

In our experience at gigCMO, the ideal gig candidate is someone who has reached a point in their career where they are no longer striving principally for personal gain. With a rich CV and knowledge gained through the hard graft of years going through the ranks, they bring integrity, trust and a seasoned outside perspective to your business in order to guide it through a particular growth phase or situation.

The most successful gig candidates to come into the C-Suite are in their 'third careers'. That is to say, they've done the groundwork, they've been in your seat surrounded by other senior executives, and they're no longer striving to build that kind of competitive momentum in their own careers. They're motivated by interesting projects, fulfilment and freedom, and when they come to your business they're not coming with ego and agenda to compete with other egos in your business. The C-Suite's gig candidate is there to support you and the things you want to achieve.

What's in it for you?

As a business owner, growth, goal acquisition and financial gain are likely to be top priorities, and so they should be. Likewise, young high fliers bring an important energy, vital to have within your midst to drive innovation and a universal desire to surge forwards. All of that needs a leveller however, to avoid making the faux pas that you could only foresee through experience, to envisage strategies and directions that only time makes you party to, and to deliver ideas and directives with an aplomb that turns aggression into assertiveness. So within your effusive, energetic, driven and likely competitive team, it's important to have a smattering of people who are ambitious for you, but who are not competing with you. That is the role of your high value gig consultants.

It is also important to consider where you as a business leader are getting your support. It's easy to think you should have all the answers, and while supporting everyone else within your team, it raises the question, who's there to support you? Having been in that position themselves, a gig CMO for example, will understand the position you're in and the challenges you face in your professional sphere, and maybe with some empathy as to the impact it all has on your personal life as well. Positive mentality and resilience are crucial elements of a successful business, and the ideal gig candidate will be empathetic to you and understand what it takes to achieve a particular goal. But now, as they're not in competition with you to get there, you benefit from mentoring, coaching and the insight and knowledge that they bring. Quietly confident and a discreet confidante.

We mentioned in Chapter 4 that a study of executive profiles by the Harvard Business Review showed that the value in the C-Suite is generally felt to be in leadership skills and a strong grasp of business fundamentals rather than in technical and functional expertise. While the intricacies of technologies get more advanced from one generation to the next, business fundamentals, and ultimately, the art of liaising with other leaders are predominantly recognised to have nuanced, core pillars of understanding and diplomacy that your gig consultant can bring. It's a high but indefinable value that their own successes attest to, but the bottom line is that it's experience led not opinion led knowhow that they bring to the C-Suite, and unless you've learned it yourself over time, the only way to get it is by getting the right quality of person into your business.

What's in it for them?

The pay off for this Holy Grail of long and hard learned business acumen that a gig consultant provides is encompassed in all the things we have spoken about so far in other chapters; lifestyle goals, freedom, and being in charge of one's own schedule.

Having reached their third career, the ideal gig candidate no longer has the desire to harp back to their big glass corner office, even if it still existed. The big pay cheques may well be tantalising, but they've got the t-shirt and they frankly don't fancy doing the daily commute to pick up another one.

The key driver for the gig candidate is to add value - this is the crucial part of the successful gig mindset. Having learned so much they want to give back and in turn feel valued for the depth of understanding that they can now bring. As we said before, these are people who have no doubt been in your shoes, knowing full well the stress, fear, excitement and workload that you're under, and they take great pleasure in helping you to balance those elements and get to where you want to go. In short, they want to put their experience to positive use, and have time to enjoy it as well. Real world expertise that brings real world benefits.

Key points

- It's about selecting the right gig candidate to bring the right mindset to your business, not just choosing any-one with a good CV and putting them on a temporary contract.
- Find gig employees who can help you to achieve your targets for your business and help to guide younger team members.
- As a business leader, where do you get your support? The right gig employee is at a stage in their career where they understand the pressures you are under, and without an agenda they can offer support to you personally as well as to your business.

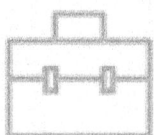

CHAPTER 6: What mindset do you need to keep your talent?

AT ITS CORE, our interpretation of the gig economy is to allow your business to benefit from the skillsets of the best talent available.

Attaining and retaining talent is an increasing headache for HR departments committed to an outdated way of operating because, as we have already mentioned, many companies are increasingly finding that there are fewer people looking to fill highly skilled roles on a full time basis.

It is a mindset that can take some adjusting to, but the changes in ways of working and individual priorities are forcing HR departments to think in a different way if they're to help your business thrive moving forward.

Talent doesn't want to be retained

March 2017 saw the fastest decline in permanent candidate availability in 15 months according to a Markit/ Recruitment and Employment Confederation UK Report on Jobs, and REC Chief Executive Kevin Green commented: "Finding people to do the jobs on offer is rapidly becoming employers' biggest headache, and many are reporting an increasing number of white-collar jobs as hard to fill, including in the IT and financial sectors."[26] In light of that, one has to consider, if the system's broke, why not find an alternative?

Those two elements - 1) the decline of permanent roles and 2) a lack of suitable candidates, is precisely the driver for the gig economy, which provides a solution to both problems. Employee mentality has changed as a result of the socio-economic changes (we have already highlighted that workers are asking for different things from their jobs such as work/life balance and a higher sense of purpose compared to traditional rewards such as status and internal job progression), so the people with desirable qualifications are no longer seeking permanent positions.

The nature of transition, is that there is a natural degree of resistance to change, and in particular it seems that HR departments have been wrestling with the value proposition in their businesses that encompass both permanent and impermanent people. There are question marks over how to create and keep a company culture that serves customers, whilst also supporting both transient and full time employees, not to mention a comparatively unknown measurement as to their effectiveness alongside the longer-term tribe.

All of this is entirely understandable except for two things. First, is that the gig economy is a model that's growing having been pioneered amongst some of the fastest growing and successful businesses of the post-recession age. It's a model used by Silicon Valley's golden children and not without reason. The second is that HR departments have been clinging to the idea of retaining talent. However, the short of it is that you can't retain it because economic change and political upheaval have lead to an evolution in the way we think about work

---

[26] http://www2.staffingindustry.com/eng/Editorial/Daily-News/ UK-Permanent-candidate-availability-drops-at-fastest-pace-in-15-months-41630

both as individuals and as businesses. So not only does talent not want to be retained in the same way as before, but you don't want to retain it either. What you do want to do want is more skilled and nuanced than that.

The changing role of HR departments

To understand the changing role of HR departments, we need to start by thinking about how we define our employees. Do you think of your contractors and temporary staff differently from permanent, full time employees? Once upon a time contractors were almost second class citizens in organisations but that has definitely changed - it has had to, with around 4.7 million self-employed workers in the UK and counting[27]. We have to start thinking holistically about recruitment in order to attract and retain talent from all angles.

A lot has changed in HR over the last decade, let alone the last 20 years. Processes have been turned on their heads and the methods of recruiting have been completely altered with the rise of digital platforms including LinkedIn and HR Charlie. Crucially however, the expectations have changed from both sides, and as a result what we have is no longer a static formula but a dynamic ecosystem of skills from which to draw. It's no longer about making people fit a mould, but adapting the mould to get the right person for the job and part of that means buying talent in as you go along.

With these increasing changes, the metrics by which success is measured must also change. Jim Barnett, CEO of Glint, a maker of employee engagement software told fastcompany.com: "Traditional metrics will need to be tweaked in order to properly measure these workers in terms of engagement and retention," continuing. "This will require significant gains in speed and agility in order to quickly identify work/projects in need of atten-

[27] http://www.telegraph.co.uk/news/2017/03/10/britains-self-employed-army-keeping-economy-afloat/

tion, source employees with the required skills, and staff project teams that can quickly perform the necessary task."[28]

To a great extent over recent years, HR departments have been caught napping, with their out of date mindset forcing their companies to grapple with the now and face an uncertain future. The Office of National Statistics has said that self employment has been one of "the defining characteristics of the UK's [post recession] economic recovery,"[29] making it just one of the indicators that this changing trend in recruitment is not going to stop any time soon.

The result is that businesses need to think of themselves as part of an ecosystem rather than an isolated entity. So what HR departments now need to do is think about the future of their company, looking at how to both attract talent in all its constituent parts and also to consider how they create a culture that supports both the permanent employee looking for a steady environment as well as contract workers adapting to an ever changing one. In short, you don't choose the talent any more, the talent chooses you.

Re-evaluating your employee value proposition

"There is no talent shortage," says Forbes, "only poor recruiting practices... recruiting problems are operational problems on the employer's side — not deficiencies in the talent community!"[30] One of the key points that they highlight is that successful job ads speak to real

[28] https://www.fastcompany.com/3066905/how-the-gig-economy-will-change-in-2017

[29] http://www.telegraph.co.uk/news/2017/03/10/britains-self-employed-army-keeping-economy-afloat/

[30] https://www.forbes.com/sites/lizryan/2017/03/11/five-ways-your-recruiting-process-drives-talent-away/#116b91d8789f

people rather than dream people, and herein we can read elements such as work/life balance.

Where once upon a time the head hunter was an omnipotent force in the business world, today there is an in increasing amount of control in the hands of the employee/contractor. In this ecosystem of talent, the key factor for your business is making it attractive enough for that talent to choose to come and work for you over anyone else. That means re-evaluating the employee value proposition, your value chain, strategies, systems, processes, culture, benefits and overall stickiness with consideration of both the present and future goals of your organisation.

It is not to say that where we are today is exactly where recruitment is going to be in two, five, 10 or 20 years' time, but what we are seeing is a seismic shift in the way both businesses and individuals work and that requires a change in mindset when it comes to how we think about talent and how we bring it into our organisations. It is more fluid, more dynamic and that is an exciting place to be - the question is, are you and your HR department considering how you're going to manage those changes?

Key points

- How are you adapting your business to attract talent to your organisation?
- Reconsider your employee value proposition (EVP) for a new generation of employees.
- How are you and your HR department working to create and retain a company culture that serves customers and supports both transient and full time employees?

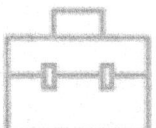

CHAPTER 7: Where is the gig economy going?

IT'S IMPORTANT to remember that economic life-cycles ebb and flow and rarely reach a final destination. Nor can we see into the future. The gig economy is a phenomena that has already changed dramatically in the time that it has become more recognised and prevalent and it will continue to evolve - that is its strength. What is happening represents a seismic shift in the way we work, but what is really important about it is how it impacts our thinking about the way we work.

We have talked about the gig mindset in terms of an employee perspective and a company perspective; the type of thinking it takes to make it work in senior level roles and what it means for company structure. Key to that is an openness and preparation for how the gig economy will continue to change the way we work.

There are a lot of assertions made about where the gig economy will take our working culture in the future. Change is often daunting but the truth is that there has been a rapid evolution of skillsets already in certain industries where work can be disaggregated in a supply chain. The gig economy has a mindset of its own, and while your own company strategies refine the nuances of that within your brand, it is not a lack of company culture that it engenders, but a more fluid one, a different approach, perhaps a broader understanding of your company's place in a wider ecosystem where employees expect impermanence rather than long-term stability

Marketing is the perfect space for a gig evolution

Marketing is already accustomed to changing flavours of in-sourcing, outsourcing, disaggregated supply chains and the impact of technology all of which have accelerated the evolution of the skillsets required in the future CMO. Already out of date is the model of one lead strategic agency with a world of creatives, who are generally beyond the reach of you (the client), to do the leg work. You would have been reliant on this large specialist resource to find the right creatives for your brief without being party to the inner workings of the process which often includes freelancers. In reality, the creative industry is already used to a gig style of working and adapting to new tasks, projects and working environments.

Now we are seeing the (marketing) client engage directly with smaller agencies, individuals and platform owners (Google, Facebook etc) and that is a trend that's set to continue.. You are no longer at the beck and call of other agencies; you bring in different skills at different times, whether that be copywriting, social media expertise, brand design, web or SEO. Precisely because of this specialist sourcing - this is where the gig CMO role can be crucial.

Where historically the CMO had a peer relationship with that big agency, you now need someone who understands the whole gamut of marketing elements - when you need them, how you need them, and most importantly, how to aggregate those skills and individuals to deliver a targeted marketing strategy. In short, the experienced eye of someone who can see the bigger picture, create the business strategy and pull together the disparate disciplines into a coherent and integrated approach to the market.This is where the model has fallen down for many; in not understanding how to manage this new style of workforce.

It's important to understand that 'autonomy' for the gig worker does not equate to 'working in isolation'. And because you are no longer outsourcing to one big agency, you need big brain skills to effectively coordinate both your needs and the needs of the people you recruit permanently and temporarily to deliver your business goals.

Will AI destroy the need for a human workforce?

No, at least not in our lifetime. As all things digital get evermore intelligent it's a natural thing to imagine a dystopian world where computers have taken over, but that way of thinking is a little reductive. Where technology is magnificent, is that it helps us to gather data, monitor and implement ideas against a plethora of factors that would have been entirely unknown 20 years ago. Faster and faster.

Technology is a marvellous tool, whether it's part of your recruitment or your marketing, but it's no substitute for human interpretation and decision-making. And implementation of the technology still has a long way to go, exposing flaws in practice. Have you ever bought something online, only to discover the website advertising exactly the same item to you five minutes later (and for the next week)? The technology is doing exactly what it should be doing - monitoring your behaviour - but the process (where AI and human intervention come together) hasn't yet caught up. You've just been to Kuala Lumpur so you're not looking for deals to go again any time soon!

So your marketing strategy extends not only into the material that you market and the tools you use, but to the people and their way of working as well.

Up-skilling in the gig economy

For the individual gig worker, the question of remaining relevant and current in the marketplace is key - as being able to provide sought-after skills increases employability.   Meanwhile, for companies, the question of how to up-skill your staff has always been costly and time consuming, particularly in this increasingly fast paced world of marketing.

Less and less organisations can afford ongoing training programmes for their people.   Given this trend it would be easy to wonder how individuals in the gig economy remain at the top of their game with their transient working lifestyles, but in actual fact, this way of working is key to their competitive edge, and is an inherent part of the sharing economy culture.

People who have chosen to work in the gig way know their livelihoods depend on them staying relevant and skilled, so they are motivated to purposely keep themselves up to date and seek out opportunities to up-skill.

The second important point is that by dint of working with different people, with different ideas, in different companies and with different technologies all the time, they really do learn on the job. Faith Popcorn, CEO and founder of Faith Popcorn's BrainReserve explained it to fastcompany.com as "a tech-enabled, nomadic existence in which there's a constant mix of business and pleasure."[31]

So in addition to their ideas, the practical skills that they bring to your company are invaluable.   They are more likely to know the pitfalls and benefits of new concepts because they may well have just been implementing them and learning them elsewhere. Being part of this ecosystem of recruitment makes for a more beneficial and cost effective learning process for you and your company.

---

[31] https://www.fastcompany.com/3066905/how-the-gig-economy-will-change-in-2017

The result is that trends in the gig economy are heading towards a world with a more cost effective flow of high level skills, a more strategic and targeted way of working, and results delivered at lower cost, lower risk and better value.

Key points

- As AI and robotics become increasingly prevalent, how are you going to create meaningful human endeavour within your organisation? Consider the human skills needed to make your business flourish.
- How do you continue to bring new skills into your organisation? Gig workers are self motivated to keep their skills up to date and ahead of the curve.
- Benefit from the ecosystem of high level skills within the shared economy to bring new ideas to your organisation.

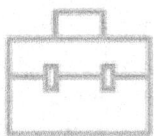

CHAPTER 8: Risk and the entrepreneurial age

THE GIG ECONOMY is an exciting place to be and with it comes a whole new dawn of opportunities and change. What gigCMO proposes is not to have an answer to every question but to provide a method by which you can bend, flex and flow with inevitable change in working culture.

Of course, we are not the only ones who will have to change. If the way we work and recruit changes, then so too must the way we manage risk, insure against critical illness, fund maternity and paternity leave, look after healthcare, assess for mortgages and loans, and even define old age. Those are things that we will have to address as businesses, individuals and also at state level.

As the way in which we work continues to evolve, the way we support our workers will be exposed as fundamentally flawed. We believe the market is changing and in response, the state will have to follow.

Should we pool risk?

When is retirement age? What does it mean to be 'old'? And who's responsible for who? The boundaries between what used to be a clear way of being are changing before our eyes, and so too must the way we respond. If you apply for a mortgage you need to demonstrate an income. As a bank in a world of gig workers, how will you decide what to lend? What will you do with a successful gig worker with an unstable income?

The Financial Times has reported that a number of businesses are already taking these questions into consideration and finding solutions by pooling risk. "Social insurance is one such area in which there is more room for entrepreneurial ventures as opposed to state bureaucracies," it says, citing localised French fraternal systems in the late 1800s that "could not scale up to the point where the entire population would be covered" and therefore required state management.

Of course, the reality was that the localised systems were very effective in their areas because of a sense of community. What we are seeing in some areas now is the rise of a new type of community, or what the Silicon Valley entrepreneur Balaji Srinivasan calls "cloud communities", based on people who could be geographically distant but who are very close in terms of profile and interests. [32]

Do more solutions lie in the new working ecosystem?

The article's crux was to look into the welfare state for the entrepreneurial age, and this way of thinking raises interesting questions and opportunities for us all. It's a perspective that of course has already been raised at a fairly base or negative level so far with critics?about the lack of employee rights for a gig worker, but in essence it is not a lack but a change and in many ways the full story is as yet unwritten because it is changing the fabric of how we work.

---

[32] https://www.ft.com/content/
a642d4ae-4169-11e7-82b6-896b95f30f58

We live in an ageing population with an eternally rising age of retirement. The gig economy provides a solution for employment at all levels by leaving positions open to a new generation of workers, whilst providing an effective role for more experienced members of the team in a capacity that suits them. It is another facet of a recruitment ecosystem whereby the senior gig worker balances out experience and training with younger, next generation team members - so you have the energy, generational relevance and experience all integrated into workforce spanning age 18-85.

So leading on from that, is there another way this ecosystem could help us support our workers and our businesses? All workers need support at different life stages, whether expected or not. Will companies get together and create combined parental cover insurance options for themselves and their teams? Will new companies arrive and pool money to provide a level of support regardless of what situation the gig worker is in? Instead of going to a life insurance provider and a separate health insurance company, will a new company emerge where you can draw down funds when you need them and for whatever you need them for? How will the state predict tax payments over a lifetime with inconsistent peaks and troughs of work?

The truth is these are questions with no answers at the moment, but people are working flexibly because it works for both them and the businesses they want to serve, so by necessity the structures around us need to respond, both public and private.

Key points

- How are you going to support your gig workers in this changing economy as employee rights strive to catch up with changing business practices?
- A strategic use of experienced gig workers and younger team members can help balance energy, genera-

tional relevance and experience into an integrated workforce of all ages.
- Consider the opportunities to work with other organisations to support this creative pool of gig workers.

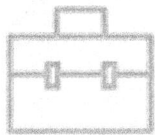

CHAPTER 9: A changing world

THE CRUCIAL THING about the gig economy is that it is very much a part of an evolution in the way that we live and work. As with every evolution, there is an element of trial and error and there can be teething problems, in this case, ones that have been widely discussed.

The basis of concern is the issue of worker rights in an unregulated method of working. From there a catalogue of details have emerged about the way in which we monitor and support individuals who choose or find themselves in a gig style of working. Many of the problems come from the way in which the gig economy came about, a conception which is rapidly evolving into something more significant, more stable and more interesting for the long term, so long as Government and mindset can adapt with it.

In a general context there is a lot of change going on. The gig economy has been described as the fourth industrial revolution and is a change that's carrying us en route to a machine oriented age of working. The pace of change for both individuals and companies is extremely challenging - keeping up with innovations and changing skillset requirements can be both daunting and draining, so it is unsurprising that there have been hiccoughs along the way for those pioneering change. "Is the gig economy working?" asks the New Yorker amidst a plethora of headlines that question its validity - well, it's evolving is really the honest answer.

Worker rights and where the gig economy started

For example, this year we have seen the likes of Uber and Deliveroo, famed advocates and literal drivers of the gig economy in its original guise, coming under fire by a parliamentary committee over the companies' working conditions[33], including job insecurity and employment rights. The criticism is not unjust as it seems it is possible for gig workers to earn well below minimum wage at the moment as they are not seen by the companies they work for as employees but contractors — though a court ruling against Uber disagreed in 2016.

This has been the big issue so far highlighted within the gig economy - the fact that our wider infrastructure is not yet fully prepared for it, and for this reason some employers have fallen foul of employment laws - which is the reason to approach it with a considered proposition, ensuring you're fully informed and so too are the workers you engage. It is crucial that this way of working is done in the right way with the right kind of gig worker - a fact we have already touched upon in previous chapters.

The concern over worker rights lead to the Taylor Review in July 2017 which calls for a new category of worker, which gives those in the gig economy some employment benefits and ensures a decent wage.[34] Given the rapid growth of this way of working and the increasingly white collar implementation of the practice, it is reliably projected that this is a big part of the future of work, and so governmental and institutional change is required in order to stem both real and feared problems with it. After all, do we want to build a future in which either perceived or practical job insecurity is a significant factor?

Perhaps one of the biggest misconceptions about the future of the gig economy, which again stems largely from its genesis, is that it is about app-based platforms that dole out work in bits and pieces. We have already progressed beyond with both more traditional businesses employing on the gig basis, as well as more of a contractor style of working being part of the gig landscape. Meanwhile, zero hour contract working has been lumped into the emerging gig economy, having its place as part of the changing way of working - paid

---

[33] https://www.theguardian.com/business/2017/jul/25/uber-deliveroo-chiefs-grilling-mps-gig-economy-self-employment

[34] http://www.wired.co.uk/article/what-is-the-gig-economy-meaning-definition-why-is-it-called-gig-economy

hourly, but with no set minimum - part of companies trying to cut or limit staffing costs.

The need for meaningful human endeavour

Meanwhile the machine age looms large as AI and robotics threaten the way we not only work but also the skills required at work and the way we perceive our working lives. As algorithms are developed that can write articles indistinguishable from those written by people, and machines can take over tasks such as administration and even moving into white collar roles, the quest for meaningful human endeavour raises a catalogue of questions. For example, what will be the disruptive impact of driverless vehicles considering that driving is the single largest occupation of US men today?[35]

Again, Uber sits ready and waiting as a pioneering example having launched the first fleet of driverless cars in Pennsylvania - an interesting move that places it ahead of the curve with major competitors and industry leaders technologically. The human role will move from driver to technician.[36] Meanwhile, big corporations such as EY have taken the changing demands of world business and have identified the future skills that are in demand in the world moving forward, which include problem solving, creativity, cognitive flexibility, emotional intelligence and collaboration - inherently human skills in effect.[37]

The changing perception of the gig economy

The problems with the gig economy are not things to sweep under a rug and forget about. For all the flexibility it brings, there are those who say the roles "aren't as flexible as they seem, as workers are incentivised or pressured to work when the companies need them."[38] It is true to note that

[35] http://www.ey.com/gl/en/issues/business-environment/ey-megatrends-future-of-work

[36] http://www.telegraph.co.uk/business/2016/09/14/watch-uber-launches-driverless-car-service/

[37] https://ukcareers.ey.com/graduates/futureskills

[38] http://www.wired.co.uk/article/what-is-the-gig-economy-meaning-definition-why-is-it-called-gig-economy

some companies have taken the opportunity to seemingly be both negligent and exploitative in their employment approaches - for example, Hermes was accused of failing to pay the minimum wage to delivery drivers operating on a gig basis. However, it is not a case that 'gig' should become a byword for exploitation, as it begins to broaden and deepen as a concept, with new versions of it appearing all the time.

The things that are negative, frightening, problematic and incomplete in terms of formal process however, are the same things that herald a time of opportunity and innovation. The gig economy is not the final destination in changing world business, but the skills and processes that we develop within it are destined to be be a vital part of the roadmap moving forward.

More importantly, the gigCMO approach is not part of the gig economy's past but its progressive future - the changing perception and the new way in which it can be used to benefit both individuals at a certain stage in their career, and companies in need of experienced input.

Key points

- There are many businesses that have fallen foul of employment laws with gig workers, highlighting the importance for a carefully considered HR policy.
- Look to the future and consider how changing robotics and AI will alter your company's needs in order to create meaningful human endeavour.
- It's important to think of the gig economy as part of an ongoing change in the way we work, and an opportunity for you and your HR department to reconsider future policies.

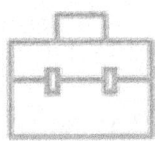

CHAPTER 10: How attractive are you?

WHILE WE'RE all very good at considering the microcosm that is our own economic and political sphere, what the gig economy is presenting us with is a wider, more fluid and flexible world of working where the key is in being an attractive employer for this new kind of worker.

We have established that we are no longer talking about a world of big glass corner offices and conventional rewards. When we talk about being attractive it has to come in real value for the individual - achievement, purpose and quality of life, and that requires businesses to embrace a whole new mindset that starts in their HR department.

We have mentioned an 'ecosystem', but we need to understand that concept intrinsically, not merely academically. Its veins have to run through all aspects of the business rather than a buzzword to trot out at corporate meetings or a box checking exercise.

At the heart of it all, your business needs to make itself attractive to the market workforce in a way the workforce has previously become accustomed to making itself

attractive to prospective employers. How are you reimag-
ining your business for the gig economy?

Attracting talent

The confluence of the fast pace of technological
innovation, increasing customer demands and evolving
expectations of the work environment means that the
whole model of how we work is adapting. It is predicted
that by 2020 40% of the employees in your company will
be on some form of temporary contract - a fact inconceiv-
able 20 years ago. Your decision to either take that trend
by the horns and make it work for you, or to be dragged
along in its wake will impact how your business is seen
and how it functions moving forward.

Firstly, we're no longer talking about employees,
we're talking about 'talent'. Can you look at your business and see why it is or is not attractive to the kind of
talent you want to attract? The role of HR is changing
and key to its future is looking at your Employee Value
Proposition (EVP) and upping your pulling power. Within
this you will need to consider how attractive your office
culture is to both those who are permanent and those
who are transient. Indeed, how do you create an office
culture at all?

Historically, the weight of employment has been on
the employee looking for a job, but that weight is being
placed back on the employer to compete for the people
they want in the jobs they have available. The make-up
of the workforce is going to look increasingly different -
there will be requirements for jobs that haven't even been
invented yet and skills you don't yet know you will need.
How do you start looking for that when you don't even
know what you're looking for? How do you prepare to
access that before there is a mad rush to get it? How do
you make sure there is an organic flow of talent into your
business, making your company a desirable place to
work whilst also encouraging a healthy flow both ways?

As gigging becomes evermore common, it is not going to be enough to look at your contractors and think that a lucrative pay cheque is enough to attract them. These people are not your second class citizens, they are key drivers in your business - a lifeline of skills and ideas that ebb and flow. Consider the rewards, what these people are looking for and how to help them find you in a market of increasing opportunity.

Step outside yourself to see the new competitors

Airbnb, Uber, LendingClub - these are the companies that have embraced the sharing economy and have blown traditional competitors out of the water. The chances are that your greatest competitors don't even exist yet, and the key to longevity (as we know) is adaptability. Remember what happened to Kodak?[39] The photography oligarch wilfully ignored the rise in digital photography and ended up filing for bankruptcy in 2012 while their rivals at Fuji invested in new technology and diversification into new businesses. It has taken nearly 5 years but Kodak has since re-invented itself in printing and packaging solutions. But what a different turn the company has had to take in a new ecosystem as a different kind of brand.

There are two prongs to this need for flexibility - the first is in listening to your customers. The second is making sure you have the skills to understand what they want and deliver it to them, recognising that your greatest tools are the team around you, and to get the best you need to recognise the way they want to work. Can you step outside yourself and see what is happening in the market? Perhaps that's where your experienced gigCMO can first begin to add value - by seeing your business from a different perspective without being blindsided by past or even current successes.

---

[39] https://leaderonomics.com/business/kodak-vs-fujifilm-success-failure

Diversity is different

Diversity was one of the defining challenges of the 20th century workforce, but we're no longer talking about it in the context of sex or race, we're talking about it in terms of demographic, skillsets and ways of working.

Businesses are seeing a new type of diversity forming the make-up of their workforces as they analyse the requirements of particular roles; this diversity is a fusion of gig working integrated alongside other types of working. We're not talking about boxes for people to fit in at different stages of their careers and lives, we're talking about the company that reimagines roles and opportunities to meet the talent requirement of business, and the work/life requirements of the individual.

The demographic is also changing. In an ageing society we can no longer realistically rely on retiring at the age of 60 and frankly many of us don't want to. We enjoy our work, we get a lot out of it. Contrary to popular opinion it isn't just about the money (although for many the concept of retirement is simply unaffordable no matter how successful we are).

This 'older' workforce has a valuable place in business. They do not take away from those new to the market, but are poised to add long term value to their careers as well as the businesses they serve when positioned effectively by employers. Gig workers such as a gigCMO have the time, experience and understanding to nurture younger talent for the long term value of a brand - a vital part of this ecosystem of shared skillsets and constant learning that is 100% necessary in a world of eternal change.

Consider how you are going to support your coveted gig worker who also happens to have a family or lives in another country? How are you going to integrate an incoming workforce of young and dynamic but less experienced creatives alongside ageing but pricelessly talented pros? Remote working, flexible working and tailored solutions are no longer optional extras, they are a significant section of your workforce and the difference between the outdated and the future proofed, the fat and complacent vs the lithe and agile organisation.

The gig mindset - have you got it?

All of this is part and parcel of embracing the gig mindset - a potent fusion of accountability and affordability at all stages. It is about making the employee minutes and office square footage work for their place in the budget. A more flexible workforce supported by remote access technology helps answer society's increasing issues of economic and environmental sustainability, but it requires companies to really think about the path they choose to take forward.

Key points

- What motivates your team and your employees?
- What are your goals for your business and for your career as a leader of an organisation?
- If talent doesn't want to be retained, how are you going to attract it to your organisation?
- What is your approach to the new meaning of diversity within your organisation?

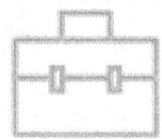

About gigCMO

GIGCMO IS A business consultancy and an innovator in the sharing economy, lead by real-world, blue chip, internationally experienced, bottom-line oriented CMO's. We come into your business on a fractional basis, which means you define how long and how often you need our marketing brains and creativity to get to work on your business challenge.

We are a new breed of global management consulting, formed by select CMOs and CROs to support C-Level executives in driving their agenda for growth in marketing, technology, sales, board advice, market access and consulting.

What we do at gigCMO: We provide the key skills and amount of time you need from a CMO at a fraction of the cost of a permanent hire. In short, we work with your team and solve your business problems.

About the gigCMO team: Team members are all highly qualified with extensive international experience. When you partner with gigCMO you get the support of people with hard-earned industry reputations and extensive international experience.

Who gigCMO serves: We specialise in providing C-suite brains for organisations and companies who don't need or cannot justify a full-time permanent C-suite executive, but need an injection of talent to take the business forward.

How gigCMO works: gigCMO operates on-demand. There is no costly or time consuming recruiting. We start with a business conversation so we can work with you on the best fit solution. We stay connected and work as a team to maximise our value-add.

Contact gigCMO: Our approach is personal, confidential and discreet.

gigcmo.com
+44 (0) 2081235778

cmo@gigcmo.com